Jerusalem Sky

Jerusalem Sky

Stars, Crosses, and Crescents

by Mark Podwal

A Doubleday Book for Young Readers

With wonders and miracles,

the sky over Jerusalem

touches the world below.

It lets down a ladder for angels to climb.

At midnight, it can be bright as midday.

It even knows when not to rain.

Legend says that the Jerusalem sky

has a hole in it,

made by a jewel

that fell from God's throne.

Through this hole

hopes reach heaven.

Some believe that halfway

between heaven and earth,

the Jerusalem sky

is home to a city with walls of silver,

gates of pearl, and streets of gold.

Every autumn gust tossing a leaf,

every winter cloud storming overhead,

every spring breeze rustling a treetop,

every summer rainbow promising sunshine,

is said to be born in the Jerusalem sky.

It is also said that

each morning the sun blazes red

while awakening the world

because its rays pass through

the roses on Jerusalem's hills.

Jewish sages tell how, night after night,

a full moon shone while Solomon was king.

Under his rule the Temple was built.

For the seven years it took to complete,

rain fell only after dark,

so that the work would not be delayed.

When enemies burned down the Temple,

the Jerusalem sky blew a crying wind

that scattered the Temple's stones far away.

Wherever a stone landed, a synagogue was built.

By the stones that remain, Jews still pray.

Christians tell of a wondrous star

in the Jerusalem sky,

which brightened the winter night,

announcing the news

of Jesus' birth.

And they tell how thirty-three years later,

a spring afternoon's daylight

blackened into starless night

when Jesus died on a small, jagged hill,

now crowned by a great church.

Muslims tell of the prophet Muhammad's night journey,

in which midnight glowed like day

when he rode through the sky

on a flying horse,

then reached heaven

on a stairway of light.

Where Muhammad rose to heaven

now stands a mosque

with sky blue stones

and a dome of gold

shining like a second sun.

Atop these majestic monuments to miracles,

synagogue stars,

church crosses,

mosque moons

meet under the Jerusalem sky and merge their shadows.

Jerusalem is so loved it has seventy names.

Though it is called City of Peace,

no place has been fought over more.

Seventeen times torn apart and rebuilt.

Perhaps possessing Jerusalem

is like trying to own the sky.

———

Even so, people from everywhere

every day gather in the city—

a city said to have been mapped on God's palms

long before our world began—

and with prayers for peace and miracles,

all addressed to one God,

hope lights the Jerusalem sky.

For Robert Stuart Lewis

BIBLIOGRAPHY

Goldman, Francisco (Introduction). *The Gospel According to Matthew: Authorized King James Version* (Pocket Canon). New York: Grove Press, 1999.

Séguy, Marie-Rose. *The Miraculous Journey of Mahomet.* New York: George Braziller, 1977.

Vilnay, Zev. *Legends of Jerusalem* (The Sacred Land, vol. 1). Philadelphia: Jewish Publication Society, 1973.

A Doubleday Book for Young Readers

Published by
Random House Children's Books
a division of
Random House, Inc.
New York

Doubleday and the anchor with dolphin colophon are registered trademarks of
Random House, Inc.

Visit us on the Web! www.randomhouse.com/kids
Educators and librarians, for a variety of teaching tools, visit us at
www.randomhouse.com/teachers

LIBRARY OF CONGRESS CATALOGING-IN-PUBLICATION DATA

Podwal, Mark H.
Jerusalem sky : stars, crosses, and crescents / by Mark Podwal.
p. cm.
ISBN 0-385-74689-X (alk. paper)—ISBN 0-385-90927-6 (lib. bdg. : alk. paper)
1. Jerusalem—Juvenile poetry. 2. Children's poetry, American.
3. Religious poetry, American. I. Title.
PS3566.O328J47 2005
811'.54—dc22
2004030936

The text of this book is set in 17-point Bembo.
Book design by Trish Parcell Watts
MANUFACTURED IN CHINA
August 2005
10 9 8 7 6 5 4 3 2